MUHAMMAD ALI

by
William R. Sanford
&
Carl R. Green

CRESTWOOD HOUSE
New York

Maxwell Macmillan Canada
Toronto

Maxwell Macmillan International
New York Oxford Singapore Sydney

Library of Congress Cataloging-in-Publication Data
Sanford, William R. (William Reynolds), 1927–
    Muhammad Ali / by William R. Sanford and Carl R. Green. — 1st ed.
        p. cm. — (Sports immortals)
    Includes bibliographical references and index.
    Summary: A biography of one of the world's greatest heavyweight boxers. Includes trivia quiz.
    ISBN 0-89686-739-0
    1. Ali, Muhammad, 1942– —Juvenile literature. 2. Boxers (Sports)—United States—Biography—Juvenile literature.
[1. Ali, Muhammad, 1942– . 2. Boxers (Sports) 3. Afro-Americans—Biography.] I. Green, Carl R. II. Title. III. Series.
GV1132.A44S26   1993
796.8'3'092—dc20
[B]   91-42181

Photo Credits
Cover: AP—Wide World Photos
AP—Wide World Photos: 4, 12, 14, 22, 27, 28, 32, 41
The Bettmann Archive: 9, 11, 15, 17, 19, 21, 23, 24, 31, 34, 35, 36, 37, 39, 42

Copyright © 1993 by Crestwood House, Macmillan Publishing Company

All rights reserved. No part of this book may be reproduced or transmitted in any form or by any means, electronic or mechanical, including photocopying, recording, or by any information storage and retrieval system, without permission in writing from the Publisher.

Macmillan Publishing Company   Maxwell Macmillan Canada, Inc.
866 Third Avenue   1200 Eglinton Avenue East
New York, NY 10022   Suite 200
                                     Don Mills, Ontario M3C 3N1

CRESTWOOD HOUSE

Macmillan Publishing Company is part of the Maxwell Communication Group of Companies.

Produced by Flying Fish Studio

Printed in the United States of America

First edition

10 9 8 7 6 5 4 3 2 1

CONTENTS

THE START OF A BRILLIANT CAREER

The skinny 12-year-old boy was out to have some fun. He did not know his life was about to change that day in October 1954. With a friend riding next to him, Cassius Clay cruised through Louisville, Kentucky, on his new Schwinn. When they reached the yearly Home Show, the boys parked their bikes. Inside the hall, they stuffed themselves with free hot dogs and popcorn.

When the boys left the show, Cassius's bike was gone. He ran up and down the street, asking if anyone had seen it. No one could help him. At last a man sent Cassius downstairs to the Columbia Gym. "Ask for Joe Martin," the man said.

Cassius was crying when he reached the gym. But he almost forgot his sorrows when he saw what was going on there. Boxers were sparring, jumping rope and hitting the speed bag. The smell of sweat and rubbing alcohol stung his nostrils. A boy pointed Cassius toward Martin.

"Somebody stole my bike," Cassius told the man. "When I find him I'm gonna whup him."

Martin, an off-duty police officer, was the gym's boxing coach. He filled out a theft report. Then he offered to teach Cassius to fight. Without training, he warned, "you won't whup anybody." He gave Cassius a consent form for his parents to sign.

Boxing superstar Cassius Clay, better known today as Muhammad Ali

The boy went home to confess that he had lost his bike. He forgot about the gym until he happened to see a youth boxing show on television. When he saw Joe Martin talking to one of the boxers, he remembered the coach's offer. Excited now, he told his parents he wanted to be a boxer. The Clays talked it over, then signed the form. Their hope was that boxing would keep Cassius from running with the local gang.

Young Cassius did not become a champion overnight. On his first night at the gym, he jumped into the ring with an older boxer. Minutes later his nose was bleeding and his mouth was sore. His own wild punches had mostly missed their target.

Martin took over. He taught Cassius how to move his feet and how to throw a right cross. The boy was raw and clumsy, but he never quit. Six weeks later, Martin put Cassius into the ring for his first **amateur** bout.

Cassius told everyone he met that he was going to fight on TV. He also bragged that he was going to win. When fight night came, Cassius lived up to his boast. When the bell ended the third one-minute round, the judges gave him a **split decision**.

At less than 100 pounds, Cassius Clay did not look like a future champion. Even so, the young boxer was already dreaming of future triumphs. Today the world knows that skinny black kid as the great **heavyweight** boxer Muhammad Ali.

TRIVIA 1*

When sports fans voted for this century's Greatest Male Athlete in 1977, Muhammad Ali came in third. Who were the two athletes who finished ahead of him?

* Answers to all Trivia Quiz questions can be found on page 47.

BORN TO BE A CHAMPION

The boy who grew up to become Muhammad Ali was born in Louisville, Kentucky. The date was January 17, 1942. His parents named him Cassius Marcellus Clay, Jr. Clay was a famous name in Kentucky. Long before the Civil War ended slavery, abolitionist "Cash" Clay had freed his own slaves. The great U.S. senator Henry Clay ran for president in 1832 and 1844.

Cassius Marcellus Clay, Sr., was an artist who made his living as a sign painter. He loved his family but often drank too much. Cash blamed racial prejudice for his lack of success. Once, young Cassius bragged to his father that he would be rich someday. Cash shook his head and pointed to the boy's black skin. "Only hard work will bring you success," Cash said.

Cassius's mother, Odessa Grady Clay, was young and pretty when her son was born. As a child, Cassius called his mother Bird. Odessa explained, "He says I looked like one—pert and pretty." Bird kept house at 3302 Grand Avenue in the city's west end. The house had a leaky roof and the front porch sagged. Even so, Cassius and his brother, Rudy, had toys, pets and enough to eat. When money was short, Bird cleaned houses for $4 a day.

As a baby, Cassius jabbered, "Gee, gee, gee!" Years later, he joked that he had predicted his **Golden Gloves** victories from the crib. Cassius also liked to say that he knocked out two of Bird's teeth when he was a year old. Bird shook her head when she heard that story. "Baby Cassius only loosened one tooth," she explained with a smile.

Segregation was a fact of life in Louisville in the 1940s. Blacks and whites went to separate schools and used separate rest rooms. Cassius remembers asking his mother for a drink of water while they were shopping. A store clerk refused to give the boy a paper cup of water.

Cassius was a show-off even then. When he was 12, he raced the bus three miles to school. Neighbors thought he did it to show off. Cassius claimed he ran to get in shape. Only later did he admit that the family could not afford to pay his fare. Often, he ran in secondhand shoes lined with cardboard.

The Clays wanted their son to become a lawyer or a teacher. In truth, young Cassius was not a scholar. He had a quick wit, but he never mastered the art of reading. Math was forever a mystery to him. As a result, Cash and Bird were pleased when Cassius showed promise as a boxer. Soon Cash was telling his friends that Cassius would be the heavyweight champion someday.

Cassius was consumed by the desire to excel. He studied boxing the way some people study music or art. Joe Martin and Fred Stoner taught him footwork and punching skills. Already lightning fast, his punches now came hard and straight. Proud of his body, he trained hard and refused to smoke or drink.

The long hours of training began to pay off. By the time he was 18, Cassius won over 100 amateur fights. Only eight losses marred his record. By then, he was anxious to make some money in the ring. Joe Martin told him to wait. "Win the Olympic gold medal before you turn pro," Martin advised.

TRIVIA 2   What was Muhammad Ali's lifetime record in the ring?

BOXING FOR OLYMPIC GOLD

In 1960, Cassius Clay was a tall, handsome 18-year-old. With all his energy focused on boxing, his high school classwork suffered. He graduated that spring even though he ranked near the bottom of his class. The low grades did not worry Cassius. His record proved that he had a future in the fight game. Among his trophies were two national Golden Gloves titles.

The **Olympic trials** were held in San Francisco that year. At first, Cassius refused to go. Fearless in the ring, he was afraid of flying. At last he agreed to go—and was terrified when the plane was tossed around by a storm. At the trials he fought his way into the finals, where he was almost upset. After being knocked down he stormed back to score a **TKO**. Cassius, 178 pounds and still growing, made the Olympic team as a light heavyweight.

The 1960 United States Olympic Boxing Team. Cassius Clay is standing at the back of the lineup.

A train carried Cassius home to Louisville. If he had to fly to Rome for the Olympics he would not go, he announced. Joe Martin talked sense to his star pupil. "Winning the Olympics will mean more dollars when you turn pro," the coach said. The lure of fame and big **purses** helped Cassius conquer his fear of flying.

Once he reached Rome, Cassius became an Olympic star. His speed, fancy footwork and hard punching won the hearts of boxing fans. *Sports Illustrated* picked him as the American most likely to win a boxing gold medal. When Cassius loudly agreed, no one seemed to mind.

Reporters found Cassius easy to interview. He was always "on," smiling and joking. A communist newsman tried to cause trouble by asking about racial problems at home. Cassius did not fall into the trap. "To me, the U.S.A. is still the best country in the world, including yours," he said.

Cassius enjoyed the Olympic Village. After his workouts he relaxed with the other athletes. If there was a dance, he was certain to be there. But when the boxing started, he was ready.

In his first fight, Cassius beat a Belgian boxer. In his second, he sent a Russian home with two black eyes. The third fight was closer, but Cassius won a hard-fought decision over an Australian. The win put him into the finals against a Pole named Ziggy Pietrzkowski. At 25, Ziggy was a three-time European champion. He was as hard to beat as his name was to pronounce.

At first, Ziggy's **southpaw** style confused Cassius. The Pole seemed a sure winner after the first two rounds. But Cassius took charge in the third and final round. He forgot his fancy footwork and belted Ziggy with stinging **jabs** and hard rights. Only the bell saved the Pole from being knocked out. A few minutes later the judges gave Cassius the victory.

10

Cassius stands proudly among the seven Olympians who earned gold medals at Rome during the 1960 Olympics.

Cassius stood straight and tall as the band played "The Star-Spangled Banner." He was proud of the gold medal that hung around his neck. For a time he wore it everywhere—even to bed.

The nation turned out to greet its Olympic hero. Cassius toured New York City, wearing his team jacket and his medal. Fans took him to fine restaurants and bought gifts for his family. Back in Louisville, the city celebrated with a parade. Cassius recited a poem for the crowd:

"To make America the greatest is my goal.

So I beat the Russian and I beat the Pole."

It was his first published poem. It would not be his last.

"I AM THE DOUBLE GREATEST"

Cassius was ready to turn pro when he came back from Rome. He had tasted fame and the good life that went with it. Now he wanted more.

Turning pro, he learned, was not a simple matter. A professional boxer needs a manager to arrange his fights. He needs a trainer to keep him in top shape. And he needs money to live on while he fights his way up the ladder.

Boxers Rocky Marciano and Archie Moore offered to manage the young prospect. So did Cassius's old coach, Joe Martin. Cassius said he needed "top-notch" people to guide him. With his father's help, he worked out a deal with some rich Louisville men. The men agreed to pay him $10,000 up front, a weekly salary and all his training costs. In return, Cassius agreed to pay them half of his earnings for the next six years.

Success did not change the hard facts of racial injustice. Despite his fame, Cassius still was barred from most Louisville restaurants. To the men who were paying him, he knew, he was only an exciting hobby. Bitter and unhappy, he threw his gold medal into the Ohio River.

Cassius stepped into a pro ring for the first time in October 1960. His opponent was Tunney Hunsaker, a small-town police chief. Cassius won a six-round decision and a check for $2,000. After that, the Louisville group moved Cassius to the Fifth Street Gym in Miami Beach. They hired Angelo Dundee as trainer-manager. The veteran Dundee knew that Cassius had a mind of his own. Instead of issuing orders, he made low-key suggestions. He laughed at Cassius's pranks and helped him write his poems.

Angelo Dundee was both a friend and a trainer to Cassius Clay.   13

Dundee worked to improve his boxer's ring skills. Cassius responded by training hard day after day. Boxing was his life's work and he gave it his full attention. He loved his morning runs and the workouts with **sparring partners**.

In two months, Cassius won four fights in Miami Beach—all by knockouts. He was maturing into a six-foot three-inch fighting machine. Many heavyweights are big, slow men. Not Cassius. At 215 pounds he had blinding speed and a knockout punch. He was also working hard at being a showman. Boxing fans came out to see if the Louisville Lip could live up to his boasts.

The victories came one after another. Cassius won eight fights in 1961, six more the next year. With his winnings he bought a new house for his parents. For himself he bought a black Cadillac. In late 1962 he signed to fight Archie Moore, the aging ex-champ. Cassius wrote a poem before that bout:

"When you come to the fight, don't block the door,
'Cause you'll all go home after round four."

Cassius stayed true to the words in his poem when he knocked out ex-champ Archie Moore in the fourth round of this fight in 1962.

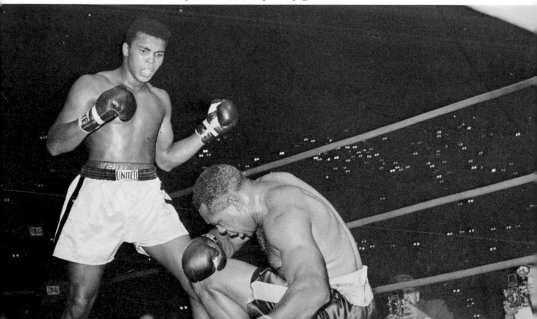

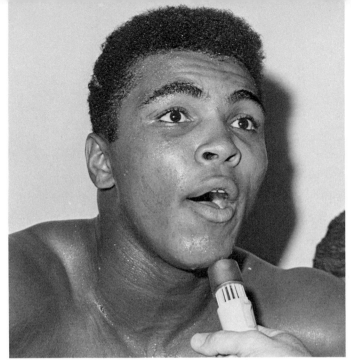

Cassius boasts to reporters after his success in the ring against Archie Moore.

Cassius kept his word. He knocked Moore out in the fourth round.

The scene then shifted to London. "This is no jive, [Henry] Cooper will go in five," Cassius sang. But Cooper's powerful left hook put the American on the canvas in the fourth round. After that scare, Cassius bounced back to score a fifth-round knockout.

"I'm not the greatest," Cassius crowed. "I'm the double greatest! Not only do I knock 'em out, I pick the round."

Sonny Liston was heavyweight champion. Could anyone beat the ex-convict with the sledgehammer fists? Cassius announced that he could. He demanded a title fight.

TRIVIA 3

Angelo Dundee, Muhammad Ali's longtime trainer and friend, saw all of Ali's great fights. What fight does Dundee point to as Ali's finest victory?

CROWNING A NEW CHAMPION

After Sonny Liston knocked Floyd Patterson out twice, experts said no one could beat him. The same experts looked at Cassius and frowned. Clay can run, they said, but he can't hide.

Liston smiled after his title fight with Cassius was set for February 1964. "A prize fight is like a cowboy movie," he said. "There has to be a good guy and a bad guy....Only in my cowboy movie, the bad guy [Liston] always wins." Gamblers agreed with him. Liston was favored to win by odds of 7-1.

As always, Cassius put on a show. Whenever Liston appeared in public, the **challenger** was there to taunt him. He called the champ the big ugly bear. One night he drove to Liston's house in Denver and shouted insults from the front lawn.

With Liston heavily favored, ticket sales lagged. Most fans thought the champ would make short work of Gaseous Cassius. Only Cassius and his close friends believed he had a chance. One of those friends was Malcolm X, a **Black Muslim** religious leader. Malcolm stayed with Cassius the week of the fight.

Cassius saved his wildest show for the **weigh-in** the day of the fight. Since heavyweights do not have to make a weight limit, their weigh-ins seldom make news. But Cassius changed all that. He charged in yelling, "Float like a butterfly, sting like a bee. Round eight to prove I'm great. Bring that big ugly bear on."

TRIVIA 4 Muhammad Ali played football as a child but soon gave up the sport. Why did he quit?

Liston held his tongue. An angry **boxing commission** stepped in and fined Cassius $2,500 for his outbursts. A doctor took his pulse. It was racing at 120 beats a minute. Clay is "scared out of his mind," the doctor announced.

That night, Cassius calmly watched his brother, Rudy, win his first pro fight. Then it was time to put on the gloves. A doctor checked his pulse. It was a steady 64.

Liston surged forward when the bell rang, ready to end the fight quickly. Cassius danced away from the champ's left hook. Next to the fleet-footed Cassius, Liston looked painfully slow. A moment later the butterfly turned into a bee. Cassius threw a flurry of crisp punches that opened a cut under Liston's eye. As the angry Liston tired, he became an easy target.

Sonny Liston lies sprawled on the floor as Cassius Clay dances around the ring shouting, "I am the greatest!"

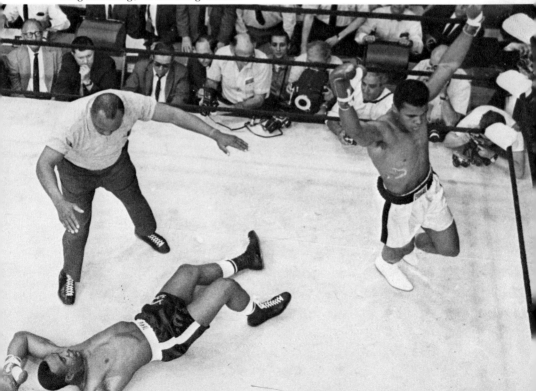

Despite his fast start, Cassius almost quit. Liston's trainers had been treating his sore shoulder with a strong salve. During round four the salve rubbed onto Cassius's forehead and dripped into his eyes. Between rounds he screamed that he could not see. "Daddy, this is the big one," Angelo Dundee snapped. He pushed Cassius back into the ring. If he had waited a second longer, the referee would have given the fight to Liston.

Cassius blinked and dodged as he tried to stay away from Liston's fists. The champ stalked him but could not land the one monster punch he needed. Slowly, Cassius's eyes cleared.

By round six, Cassius was himself again. He took command of the fight, hitting the tired champ at will. When the bell rang for round seven, Liston did not leave his stool. Torn muscles in his left shoulder had numbed his arm and hand.

Cassius danced around the ring, shouting, "I am the greatest!" Later he bragged, "Ain't nobody gonna stop me. Not a heavyweight in the world fast enough to stop me. I'm still pretty. ...The bear couldn't hurt me. I shook up the world."

Two days later, Cassius shook up the boxing world again.

TRIVIA 5

Muhammad Ali's famous battle cry "Float like a butterfly, sting like a bee" was created by one of his trainers. Who was the trainer?

"FREE TO BE WHO I WANT"

The new heavyweight champion met the press a day later. For once, Cassius did not boast about his victory. The interview was almost over when someone asked him if he was a Black Muslim.

Cassius ducked the question. He talked about the strengths of the Black Muslims and their religion. "I'm free to be who I want," he said.

What Cassius wanted soon became clear. A day later he told reporters that he was, indeed, a Black Muslim. From now on, he said, he would be known as Muhammad Ali. He had taken the new name, he added, because Cassius Clay was a "slave name."

Cassius Clay shocked the boxing world when he announced his Black Muslim faith and changed his name to Muhammad Ali.

Many Americans felt that Cassius—now Ali—had betrayed them. Whites were upset by the Black Muslim belief that blacks are superior. Beyond that fact, they knew very little about the new church. Its founder, Elijah Muhammad, was working to improve the lives of black people. He taught his followers not to dance, drink, smoke, eat pork or use drugs.

A month later, Ali went to a fight at New York's Madison Square Garden. As the heavyweight champ, he was looking forward to the cheers of the crowd. But the **promoter** told Ali that he could only be introduced as Cassius Clay. Ali turned and walked out of the Garden. The fans booed as he left.

Ali made more news in 1964. First he failed the written tests that would have made him eligible for the **draft**. "I only said I was the greatest," he smiled. "I never said I was the smartest." Then he married Sonji Roi. Sonji, a Chicago model, refused to live by Muslim rules. Instead of long robes, she wore stylish clothes. The stormy marriage lasted less than a year.

After much bargaining, Ali's backers agreed to a rematch with Sonny Liston. Liston was favored once again. Then, three days before the November fight, Ali was rushed to the hospital. After doctors repaired a **hernia**, the fight was postponed for six months.

An **assassin** killed Malcolm X three months later. The fiery black leader had left the Black Muslims to set up his own church. That same night, Ali's apartment was set on fire. People whispered that the Muslims had killed Malcolm. Malcolm's friends, the rumors said, would kill Ali to avenge their leader's death.

TRIVIA 6 When he was not training for a fight, Muhammad Ali loved to eat. He could wolf down six steaks at a sitting, but his favorite dish was served at Black Muslim restaurants. What is the dish he liked so much?

The bout was moved from Boston to Lewiston, Maine. Boston's city officials feared that someone would try to kill Ali during the fight. If there were gunmen in Lewiston, they were not quick enough. Seconds into the first round, Ali landed a perfect right to Liston's jaw. The challenger went down and stayed down. The one-punch **KO** surprised the referee, who lost track of the count.

Some writers claimed that Liston had thrown the fight. They called the knockout blow a "phantom punch." Ali ignored the abuse and began training for a fight with ex-champ Floyd Patterson.

The November 1965 fight had an ugly side. Ali had been quoted as saying, "I'm not no American. I'm a black man." Even though Patterson was also black, many whites rooted for him to "give the title back to America." The challenger further angered Ali by going along with attacks on the champ's new faith.

The fight was brutally one-sided. Each time Ali was close to knocking Patterson out, he eased up. The referee stopped the bout in the 12th round. Reporters compared the win to "pulling wings from a butterfly."

Ali made newspaper headlines when he knocked out Sonny Liston in the first round.

Muhammad Ali's radical beliefs and harsh statements caused him to lose a great deal of popularity among Americans in the 1960s.

A FIGHTING CHAMPION IS STRIPPED OF HIS TITLE

In the 1960s, the U.S. was fighting a war in Asia. At first, most Americans supported the effort to aid South Vietnam. Then, as the fighting dragged on, people began to have second thoughts. Protestors marched, chanted and called for an end to the war.

Ali's low test scores kept him out of the draft. After scoring a 16 (30 was passing), he was classed unfit for army service. His critics said he failed the test on purpose.

While the debate over his draft status raged, Ali kept busy. From March 1966 to March 1967, he defended his crown six times. Writers joked that Ali was fighting "the bum of the month."

In Toronto, Ali took on George Chuvalo. The champ gave the Canadian a boxing lesson, winning 14 of the 15 rounds. Two months later Ali fought a rematch with Henry Cooper in London. Because Cooper had floored Ali in their first fight, fans thought he might win. If Cooper did have a chance, it vanished soon after the fight started. Ali scored a sixth-round knockout.

In August, Ali barely worked up a sweat as he knocked out Brian London. A month later he flew to Germany. This was his last fight under his contract with the Louisville group. Ali made it a good one. He knocked out Karl Mildenberger in round 12.

Ali throws a jolting right to contender Brian London during this 1966 fight.

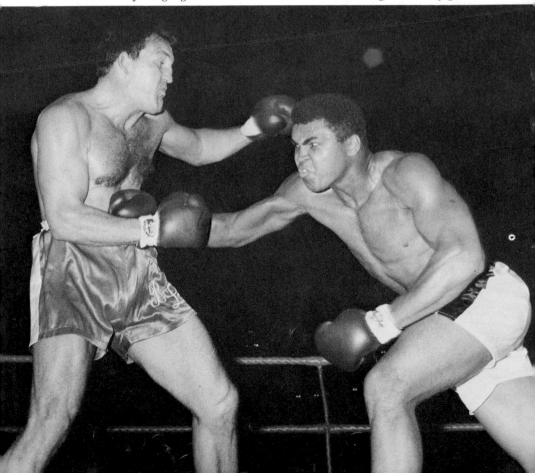

Cleveland "Big Cat" Williams was next. The challenger was a slugger whose only hope was to land one big punch. Ali refused to be hit. He taunted Williams with the "Ali shuffle," a quick little dance step. Williams threw plenty of punches but hit mostly air. Then Ali took over, rocking the Big Cat with lightning lefts and rights. Williams fell in round three.

Three months later Ali took on Ernie Terrell. For 15 rounds he punished his nearly helpless opponent. Terrell's crime? He had refused to use Ali's Muslim name. In March, Ali fought Zora Folley in Madison Square Garden. A big crowd turned out to see him beat the aging Folley in seven rounds.

Ernie Terrell throws a left punch to Ali's head. This was not enough, however, to stop the champ from winning the battle in round 15.

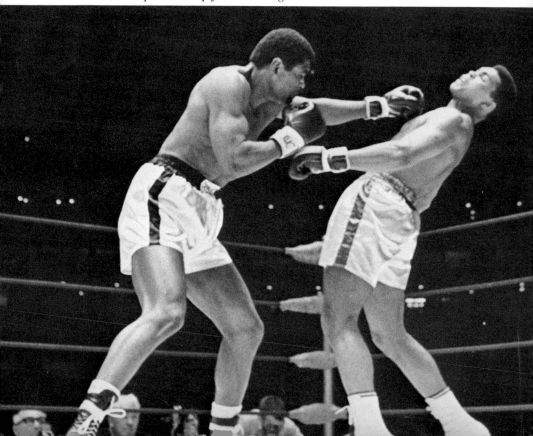

Ali lost his next fight—with his draft board. In early 1966 the passing score for draftees had been lowered to 15. Ali was moved up to 1-A, ready to be drafted. A reporter asked him what he thought of the enemy our troops were fighting in Vietnam. Ali's answer started a fire storm. "Man, I ain't got no quarrel with them Vietcong [communist troops]," he said.

Many Americans called the champ a draft dodger. Ali coolly explained that because he was a Muslim minister, he should be excused from army service. Besides, he added, he was opposed to the war on moral grounds. That was a second legal reason for refusing to be drafted.

On April 28, 1967, Ali appeared at an induction center in Houston. When his name was called, he refused to step forward. In June a jury found him guilty of breaking the draft law. The judge sentenced him to five years in jail and a $10,000 fine. Ali stayed free on bail while his lawyers **appealed**.

Ali lost more than a court case that day. The government took away his passport. The New York Boxing Commission stripped him of his title and his license to fight. Across the country, other state commissions did the same. Now Ali could not box in the U.S. and he could not leave to box overseas. It looked as though his career were over.

TRIVIA 7

In 1966, *The Ring* magazine did not name a Fighter of the Year. Why?

THE EXILE RETURNS

Starting in 1967, Ali served what he called his three-year "exile" from boxing. Denied the chance to fight, he hit the college lecture circuit. At times he spoke four or five times a week. The pay was good (up to $3,000 a speech) and the students loved him. With practice, he became a polished speaker.

Ali kept in shape by running and sparring. But without a fight to train for, workouts were not much fun. In the summer of 1967 he found some personal joy by marrying Belinda Boyd. The pretty 17-year-old took the Muslim name of Khalilah. She gave birth to the first of Ali's children, Maryum, the following June. That was also the year Ali sang in a Broadway musical.

As a pro, Ali had always spent money freely. Now, with the big paychecks cut off, he ran short of cash. A hotel manager locked him out of his room because of a $53 bill. To make some money, Ali agreed to write his life story. He wanted the book, which he wrote with Richard Durham, to set the record straight. When *The Greatest* came out in 1975 it did clear up some fables. It also added others that Ali created himself.

As the months passed, more and more Americans protested the long war in Vietnam. Sympathy began to grow for Ali and his problems with the draft. Some Georgia lawmakers helped restore his state boxing license in the fall of 1970. Ali quickly signed to fight Jerry Quarry in Atlanta. Boxing fans asked one another, "Can Ali come back at age 28?"

Jerry Quarry tries to recover from Ali's fearsome left hook.

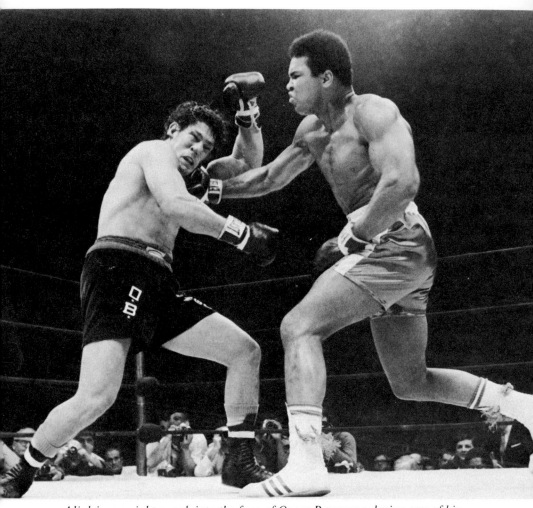

Ali drives a right punch into the face of Oscar Bonavena during one of his comeback fights in 1970.

Quarry quickly learned that the answer was yes. He fell in the third round. In December, Ali seemed his old self in beating Oscar Bonavena. Now only Joe Frazier stood between Ali and his goal of winning back the heavyweight title.

During Ali's exile, Smokin' Joe had knocked out the top contenders one by one. But he knew he had to beat Ali before he could be called the true champ. THE FIGHT, as it was billed, was scheduled for March 8, 1971. Each fighter was guaranteed $2.5 million. Never before had two unbeaten heavyweight champions met for the title. Madison Square Garden quickly sold out.

Experts thought Ali would use his jab-and-run style to wear down the bull-like Frazier. But Ali did not go into his famous shuffle. He stood his ground as Frazier planted his feet and threw his best punches. When Frazier crowded in, Ali caught most of the blows on his arms and shoulders. He also used the ropes to cushion some of the shock.

Frazier seemed to grow stronger as the fight went on. He took Ali's best shots and kept moving forward. In the 15th round the champ knocked Ali down with a crunching left hand. Ali regained his feet and held Frazier off until the final bell. Both fighters were bloody, their faces lumpy and swollen. It was no surprise when the judges gave the decision to Frazier.

TRIVIA 8

In 1962 and 1963, Muhammad Ali zoomed into contention for a shot at the heavyweight title. He fought nine times in those two years. What was notable about his record?

Writers looked at Ali's battered face and asked if he would fight again. Ali proved that he had not lost his spirit. He hollered, "Get me Joe Frazier. No man ever beat me twice."

That June, while he waited for a return match, Ali won his legal battle. Slowly, his appeal had worked its way up to the U.S. Supreme Court. When the court heard Ali's case, it threw out his conviction. Opposing war on moral grounds, the ruling said, was a valid reason for resisting the draft.

ALI TWICE WINS BACK HIS TITLE

The Muhammad Ali of the 1970s made boxing history. Some experts claimed he was slowing down, but his record denies the charge. Of his 61 pro fights, Ali fought 32 of them between 1970 and 1981. He won 27, 13 by knockouts. Along the way he regained his title, lost it—and won it back again.

After losing to Frazier, Ali had to wait three years for a new title shot. Happy to be fighting again, he kept busy. He won three bouts in the second half of 1971 and six more in 1972. Then, in March 1973, Ali ran into a buzz saw named Ken Norton. The poorly trained Ali lost a 12-round decision. He fought the last ten rounds with a broken jaw.

Six months later Ali took on Norton in a rematch. He trained harder this time. The fight was close, but Ali pulled it out with a strong finish in round 12. That win set up a rematch with Frazier in January 1974. This time it was not a title fight. Frazier had lost his crown to George Foreman.

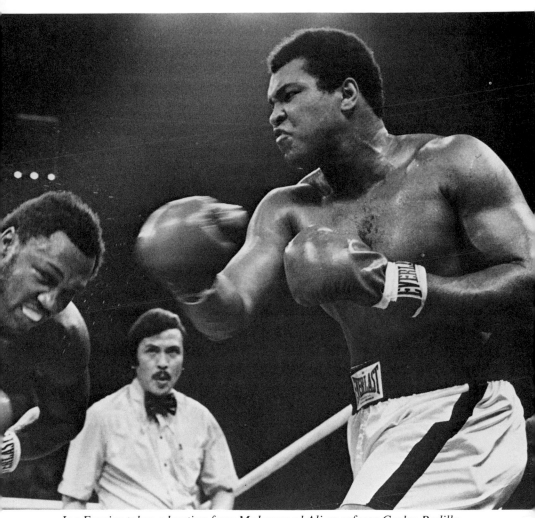

Joe Frazier takes a beating from Muhammad Ali as referee Carlos Padilla, Jr., looks on, ready to call the fight.

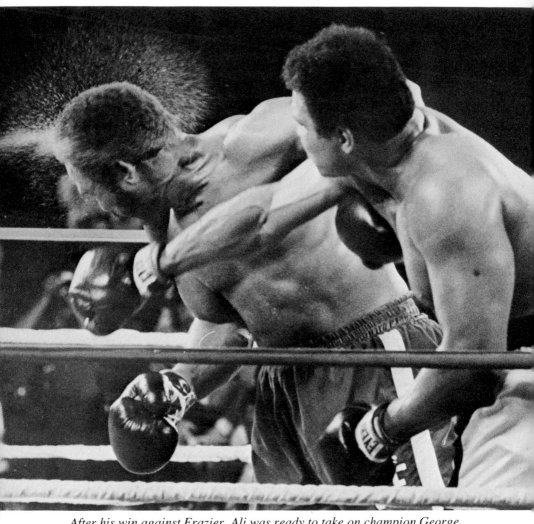

After his win against Frazier, Ali was ready to take on champion George Foreman. Foreman is shown here as he takes a stinging punch from Ali in the seventh round of their fight in Zaire.

Ali outboxed Frazier in a bruising battle. The win earned him a bout with Foreman. The match was held in the African nation of Zaire. Ali called it the "Rumble in the Jungle." Each fighter was guaranteed $5.4 million. That was more money than former champ Joe Louis earned in his entire career.

The fight started at 4:00 A.M. on October 30, 1974. The early hour put the fight on prime-time television in the U.S. Ali did not tire himself by dancing away from the giant Foreman. Instead, he backed against the springy ring ropes and absorbed Foreman's best punches. When he saw an opening, Ali lashed back with lightning lefts and rights. Foreman threw everything he had in round five, but Ali weathered the storm. "Hit harder!" Ali jeered. "Show me something, George."

Now it was the younger Foreman who looked tired. Ali stepped up his attack, rocking the champion with punch after punch. In the eighth round, Ali fired three rights and a left. Then he hit Foreman with a powerhouse right. Foreman went down for the count. It was the first time he had been knocked off his feet.

A jubilant Ali was once again heavyweight champion of the world. New York, Chicago and Louisville cheered his return. President Gerald Ford received him at the White House. Ali grinned and told the president, "Now I'm going after your job."

TRIVIA 9

After Muhammad Ali retired, he came back to fight Larry Holmes. Boxing experts knew the fight was a mismatch, but the power of Ali's name guaranteed him a big payday. How much was he paid for losing to Holmes?

In the next three years, Ali risked his title ten times. In rematches he knocked out Joe Frazier and beat Ken Norton. The champion fought in Malaysia, Puerto Rico, Germany and the Philippines. Wherever he went, crowds cheered him. He smiled as he signed autographs, posed for pictures and kissed babies.

Ali's home life was not as peaceful. Khalilah was angry because the beautiful Veronica Porche was traveling with him. The dispute led to a divorce in 1976. Ali married Veronica the following year. She later gave him two daughters.

Muhammad Ali is shown here as he greets his newest daughter, Laiya, shortly after her birth in 1977.

Leon Spinks and Muhammad Ali face the press after the 1978 fight in which Spinks became the new heavyweight champion.

The champ was slowing down and gaining weight. For his fight with Leon Spinks in 1978, Ali took it easy in training. Spinks, 12 years younger, took the title away on a split decision.

Seven months later the two met again. Ali was ready this time. He outboxed Spinks and won a 15-round decision. Now that he held the title for the third time, Ali said it was time to quit. In June 1979 he hung up his gloves.

AN ACTIVE RETIREMENT

Muhammad Ali retired from the ring but not from life. He spoke out on social problems and traveled widely. When asked, he gave his time to raise money for charity. Wherever he went people rushed forward to greet him. "Hi, Champ!" they shouted.

Retired heavyweight champ Muhammad Ali gives underprivileged kids a chance to watch him in action during a workout session.

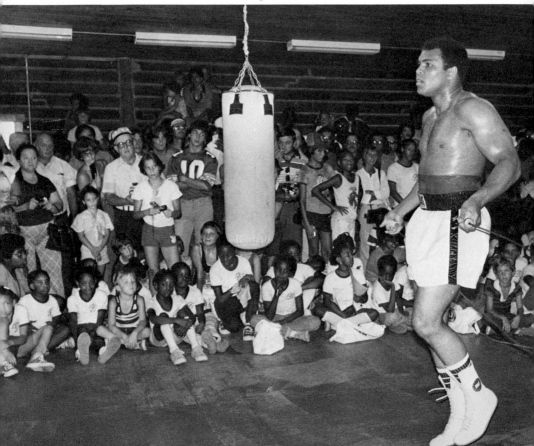

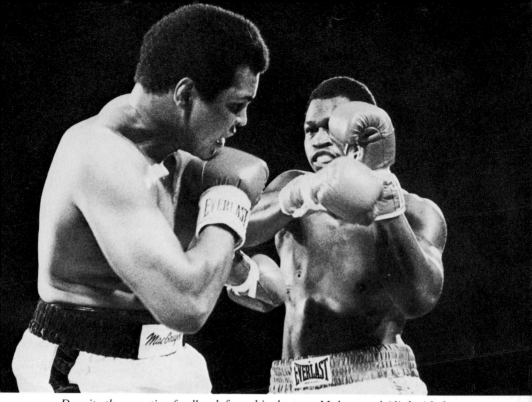

Despite the negative feedback from his doctors, Muhammad Ali decided to step into the ring again to challenge Larry Holmes. The two are shown here during the first round of their 1980 bout.

In 1980, President Jimmy Carter asked Ali to visit five African countries. Ali's job was to explain why the U.S. was not sending a team to the Moscow Olympics. In each country he asked the leaders to join the protest of Soviet aggression in Afghanistan. His hosts honored Ali but ignored his message.

In May the lure of the spotlight drew Ali back to boxing. He signed to fight his former sparring partner Larry Holmes. Ferdie Pacheco, a well-known trainer, spoke out. "Ali should not try to come back," Pacheco said. "At his age,...there's no way for him to escape the [damage] his body has undergone." To silence the protests, Ali was given a thorough checkup. Nevada's boxing commission ignored the warning signs the doctors turned up.

In training camp, Ali worked his weight down from 252 to 217. The experts began to think he might have a chance against Holmes. Then a Muslim doctor gave him some thyroid pills. The pills left Ali feeling weak. He looked good when he stepped into the ring, but he was not the boxer of old.

The weakened Ali could not defend himself. Holmes won all ten rounds before the referee stopped the fight. Only Ali's courage kept him on his feet as Holmes battered him. Doctors later said that the beating might have caused further brain damage.

Despite this sad affair, Ali climbed into the ring one last time in December 1981. If he could not win, he wanted to be throwing punches at the end. Against Trevor Berbick, he achieved that goal. Berbick beat him soundly, but Ali was still on his feet after 15 rounds.

"We all grow old," Ali said after the fight. But age was not his only enemy. In 1984 a doctor explained that Ali was suffering from **Parkinson's syndrome**. The condition explained his slurred speech and slow reactions. The doctor also made it clear that Ali was not a punch-drunk fighter. His mind was still alert.

Ali's third marriage broke up in 1986. After the divorce he married Lonnie Williams, a neighbor from the Louisville days. Lonnie looked after the champ. She made sure he ate right, obeyed his doctors and kept his appointments. Maryum Ali reported, "She really loves him and he needs to be loved."

As he settled down, Ali had more free time. He took up magic as a hobby. On his Michigan farm he spent quiet hours listening to the birds. He also found more time for his eight children.

When he's at the farm, Ali rises before dawn to say the first of

Ali recites his daily prayers among other followers of the Muslim faith.

five daily prayers. Then he signs the pamphlets he likes to hand out. In midmorning he goes for a walk to keep his weight down. After lunch and midday prayers he may visit a school to talk to the children. Following a simple dinner and sunset prayers, he watches television. Then he goes to bed.

Ali tells visitors, "People say I had a full life, but I ain't dead yet." He pledges himself to the fight against racism, crime and poverty. "My main goal now," he adds, "is helping people and preparing for the hereafter."

Few challengers were able to withstand a blow from heavyweight immortal Muhammad Ali. This photo was taken during a 1961 match with Argentinian fighter Alex Miteff.

MUHAMMAD ALI, BOXING IMMORTAL

In 1990, *Life* magazine published an honor roll of the century's greatest Americans. Muhammad Ali was one of the few athletes who made the list. As a boxer, he was honored for winning the heavyweight title three times. As an American, he was honored for standing by his beliefs during the Vietnam War.

Ali is no longer a boxer, but he still makes headlines. Late in 1990 he heard that Iraq's Saddam Hussein was holding hundreds of American **hostages**. Ali flew to Iraq to meet with the Iraqi dictator. After the meeting, Saddam released 15 Americans.

To many boxing fans, Ali is still "the Greatest." He is shown at his best in this photo as he takes Joe Frazier by TKO in a 15-round title bout.

The freed hostages saw something special in Ali. "What impressed me most…was the way he cared for everyone," one hostage said. "Inside that enormous body, I saw an angel."

Boxing gave Ali the fame that permits him to help people. Sports fans explain, "He had all the tools." Ali did have speed, power and courage—but so do many boxers. What set him apart was his ring sense. He was a genius at finding an opponent's weakness.

Who was the greatest heavyweight of all time? Among modern fighters, Jack Dempsey, Joe Louis and Rocky Marciano all have their fans. Does Ali belong on that list? He often called himself "the Greatest." Was he just running off at the mouth?

Dr. Julian Compton decided to find out. He programmed a computer with mountains of data about 24 great heavyweights. Then he matched the fighters in a **tournament**. The computer reported the results of each fight round by round.

Ali beat Jim Jeffries in his first fight. Then he outboxed Joe Louis and Jack Johnson. After those wins, the computer put him into the finals. Ali, the great boxer, faced Jack Dempsey, a rugged brawler from the 1920s.

Blow by blow, the fight unfolded. Dempsey started fast and knocked Ali down in round three. Ali shook off the knockdown and came back to floor Dempsey in the sixth. Both fighters were bleeding by this time.

The fight was close right to the end. Ali's best rounds were the 12th and 13th. Dempsey was so wobbly the referee should have stopped the fight. When the final bell rang, the scores flashed on the screen.

The referee and judges all named Ali the winner. The computer had backed up his boasts. He truly was "the Greatest."

TRIVIA 10 Even though Muhammad Ali won many fights by knockouts, he was not known for his knockout punch. What great champion won all but six of his fights by knockouts and retired undefeated?

GLOSSARY

amateur—Someone who competes for the love of sport, not for money.

appeal—Asking a higher court to retry a case that a defendant has lost in a lower court.

assassin—Someone who carries out a plot to kill a well-known public figure.

Black Muslims—A religious group that advocates the separation of whites and blacks. Black Muslims follow the rules of the Islamic faith regarding dress, diet and prayer.

boxing commission—A group of officials who control the conduct of boxing in their own state.

challenger—A boxer who has qualified to fight for the title in a particular weight class.

draft—The system set up by the government to select young men for nonvoluntary service in the armed forces.

Golden Gloves—A program that matches amateur boxers at the local, state and national levels.

heavyweight—Any boxer who weighs more than 195 pounds.

hernia—A medical condition in which internal tissue protrudes through the wall of muscle that usually contains it.

hostages—People who are held captive to secure the fulfillment of a demand.

jab—A short, straight punch used by boxers to keep opponents off balance.

KO—Boxing slang for a knockout.

44

Olympic trials—Competition held to select the athletes who will represent their country in the Olympic Games.

Parkinson's syndrome—A medical condition in which the patient exhibits many of the symptoms of Parkinson's disease. Typical symptoms include speech impairment, slowed reaction time, memory lapses and slowed movements.

promoter—The person or organization that stages a boxing match.

purse—Boxing slang for the money a boxer earns for a particular fight.

segregation—The practice of separating a minority group from facilities and opportunities enjoyed by the majority.

southpaw—A left-hander. Since most boxers are right-handed, even a great fighter sometimes has trouble with a southpaw.

sparring partner—Someone hired to box with a fighter under controlled conditions during training.

split decision—In a fight decided by a decision, the judges and the referee do not always agree. In a split decision, the winner is often chosen by a 2-1 or 3-2 vote.

TKO—Boxing slang for a technical knockout. In most TKOs, the referee ends the fight to protect a boxer who is still standing but who can no longer protect himself.

tournament—A competition in which boxers are paired off in a series of bouts. Winners advance to fight other winners, until only one winner is left—the champion.

weigh-in—The prefight ceremony in which boxers are weighed to insure that they meet the standards for their weight class.

MORE GOOD READING ABOUT MUHAMMAD ALI

Ali, Muhammad, with Richard Durham. *The Greatest: My Own Story*. New York: Random House, 1975.

Cottrell, John. *Muhammad Ali, Who Once Was Cassius Clay*. New York: Funk & Wagnalls, 1967.

Hauser, Thomas. *Muhammad Ali: His Life and Times*. New York: Simon and Schuster, 1991.

Lipsyte, Robert. *Free to Be Muhammad Ali*. New York: Harper & Row, 1978.

Mailer, Norman. *The Fight*. Boston: Little, Brown and Co., 1975.

Sheed, Wilfred. *Muhammad Ali: A Portrait in Words and Photographs*. New York: Thomas Y. Crowell, 1975.

MUHAMMAD ALI TRIVIA QUIZ

1: Jim Thorpe (football, track and baseball) finished first in the voting. Babe Ruth (baseball) finished second.

2: Ali entered the ring 228 times during his career. Of those bouts, he fought 167 as an amateur and 61 as a pro. He won 217 fights, a winning percentage of .952.

3: Dundee believes that Ali's title defense against Joe Frazier in 1975 was his greatest moment. Ali beat Frazier on a 14th-round TKO in what he called the "Thrilla in Manila." After the fight, Ali was asked what the fight had been like. He replied, "It was next to death."

4: The boxer who later took punches from Sonny Liston and George Foreman quit football because he did not like being tackled! "You got to get hit in that game," he explained. "Toooooo rough. You don't have to get hit in boxing."

5: Drew "Bundini" Brown created the battle cry while Ali was training for the first Sonny Liston fight. Brown often kept Ali loose and relaxed with his good-natured humor.

6: Ali's favorite dish was the sweet navy bean pie served at Black Muslim restaurants.

7: In 1966, Ali was clearly the best fighter in the world. But because the editors of *The Ring* did not approve of his stand on the Vietnam War, they refused to select him.

8: Of Ali's nine fights in 1962-1963, only Doug Jones went the distance with him. Of Ali's eight knockouts, six were TKOs. His average fight during that stretch ended in the fifth round.

9: Ali was paid $8 million for losing to Larry Holmes. The winner earned $3.5 million.

10: Rocky Marciano, who held the heavyweight title from 1952 to 1956, knocked out 43 of his 49 opponents.

index

921
ALI
Sanford, William R.
(William Reynolds).

Muhammad Ali.

$11.95

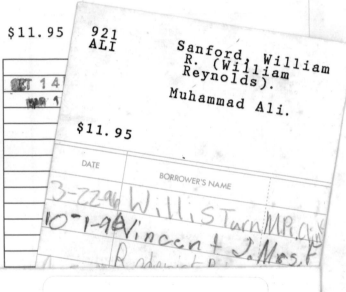

921
ALI
Sanford, William
R. (William
Reynolds).

Muhammad Ali.

$11.95

DATE	BORROWER'S NAME	
3-22-96	Willis Turn	M.P. C
10-1-9	Vincent J. Mrs. F	
	Roderick P	

ANDERSON ELEMENTARY SCHOOL
5727 LUDINGTON
HOUSTON TX 77035

BAKER & TAYLOR BOOKS